When Earth Leaps Up

When Earth Leaps Up

by Anne Szumigalski

edited with an afterword by **Mark Abley**

and a preface by **Hilary Clark**

Brick Books

Library and Archives Canada Cataloguing in Publication

Szumigalski, Anne, 1922-1999
    When earth leaps up / by Anne Szumigalski ; edited by Mark Abley ;
with a preface by Hilary Clark and an afterword by Mark Abley.

Poems.
ISBN-13: 978-1-894078-52-8
ISBN-10: 1-894078-52-7

I. Abley, Mark, 1955- II. Title.

PS8587.Z44W43 2006   C811'.54   C2006-902305-0

We acknowledge the Canada Council for the Arts, the Government of
Canada through the Book Publishing Industry Development Program
(BPIDP), and the Ontario Arts Council for their support of our
publishing program.

Cover art © CARCC. Jeannie Mah: "Eternal Knot Adrift in Blue",
porcelain, 41.5 x 15.5. x 9.0 cm., 1980.

The book is set in Bembo and Chaparral.

Design and layout by Alan Siu.

Printed by Sunville Printco Inc.

Brick Books
431 Boler Road, Box 20081
London, Ontario N6K 4G6
www.brickbooks.ca

Contents

Part 3: Day of Wings

Part 4: The Great Crocodile

Preface

by Hilary Clark

When Anne Szumigalski died in 1999, she left a hole in the Saskatchewan writing community that will never be filled. We miss her person, her ready laughter, her keen poetic ear. But we need not miss her voice, because her poems bring it to us – unmistakably, uncannily. The poems in *When Earth Leaps Up*, some published late in the poet's life and some never before published, are conduits for her precise, musical, English-accented voice. I am grateful for these poems, and to Mark Abley for gathering them together.

Like all great poets, Anne was both a creator and a destroyer. With William Blake, her familiar spirit, she knew that creation and destruction are a single process. Seeded throughout this book are clues to her poetics. In the "Statement for *A Matter of Spirit*," for instance:

> And here I am trying to plant that tree once more, trying to build that house again, the one with the angels sitting on the sill of the East window. ... They lean down and write with the fire of their fingers. ... I can only copy their words.

Planting, harvesting, building, rebuilding – in all her labours, the poet knows that what she writes is never ultimately her own and never entirely under her control. Written with fiery fingers, a poem can burn up – can burn the world up – in an instant.

In a "Statement on Peace," Anne describes her poems as "bubbles of quiet" – each bursting, replaced with another, then another – seeking "the peace of infant sleep." Yet she knows that the other side of creation is apocalypse, the infant poem "turn[ing] to shrieks angry enough to awaken the quick and the dead." Creating and destroying, the poems in this book convey Anne's poetics of last things, a "prophetics" that (like any prophet's perspective) can be most unsettling. While some may remember wonderful, warm poetry sessions at

Anne's little house in Saskatoon (and her famous scones and homemade jams), her poems themselves are rarely cosy.

Anne was very solidly of this world, yet she also looked beyond it – indeed, could pass beyond it in a blink, and look on. Perhaps this doubleness marks any serious poet. Her poems, and certainly these late poems, are marked with this double vision, a vision at once physical and metaphysical. They are full of the physical world Anne so loved: birds, cats, roses, seeds, pebbles, apples, butter & jam, juice in a cup. Yet at times these warm, soft, prickly, hard, sticky, liquid things turn ghostly, disturbed by their proximity to details beyond the normal range of experience: as when, for instance, an old woman dozing off in the warm sun sees the "unblinking" eyes of her comfortable old cat grow "huge and green ... separate planets revolving in the dark of the cat's fur" ("How strange it is ..."); or as when a boy tosses a ball in the air, his mother calling him in from the rain – "you'll catch ... your death out there" – and in the time before he catches the ball finds himself in a house which is not his own, indeed "quite other," in whose attic he comes upon an eerie girl (her neck "mov[ing] from side to side waving as gently as the stem of a crinoid, a sea lily"), a girl with the power to "claim him" ("In the park he tosses ..."). The poems are full of visions like this, little shocks suggesting that it might be easier than we think to "tear open the white envelope of time" ("A Conversation").

The themes of death and rebirth are constants, repeated with variations throughout this posthumous collection. Things are buried and things are dug up again. Partly Anne's poems touch upon the conceit, as old as poetry itself, that poems confer enduring life on their objects and thus, magically, on their author. But Anne's poems provide an ironic twist on this idea: the return to life is not always desirable. In one poem this return is figured positively, as the arrival of spring after winter: the tree of creation, Yggdrasil, "buds and blossoms with flowers // pink as cradled babies swinging / from its green and pithy branches" ("Yggdrasil"). In another poem, however, the return is not quite so sweet:

> and I tell you the sermon
> I shall give at your funeral
> "this is only the beginning
> of change" I shall say
> as I bury your pupa
> into its mound of dirt
>
> "on the day of wings
> something shall certainly emerge
> perhaps not flesh
> perhaps not what you expect"
>
> ("To a Friend Dying")

What emerges may be something neither alive nor dead: a stone heart, for instance, retrieved from a muddy ditch, "white as marble with blurred bumps of purple showing where the valves could be, and at the apex a suggestion of cut-off stumps of vein and artery ..." ("After a Fire on the Cutting – 1959"). Or memory, that zone between death and life: what emerges may be a memory of a brother's knife, "a bright blade" keenly desired and feared ("Fear of Knives"). Anne shows us that poetry brings the dead to life and suspends the living forever, but never exactly as we would expect or desire – there's always a catch, a little twist, an "Aha!"

I do hope that these late poems, these words "singing phon and antiphon into the dark" ("Taxonomy"), will delight and disturb all who read them. That's what Anne would have wanted.

Part One: The Tree of Creation

Untitled ("glory to the queen ...")

glory to the queen whoever she is
wherever she finds herself as she moves
up and down round and round
all the spaces that are hers

once she was a young thing and jumped
easily over any fence any line
now she's an old woman thick and earthy

by tomorrow she hopes to leap
out of this skin and into a new one
a skin like petals like leaves

Pompes Funèbres

once funeral hats were black cylinders
of beaver or silk and always worn
by men, bereaved women went veiled
to hide their tears or lack of them

here in the capital of winter
it's scarves across faces
grey from the frozen air
faces as dry as winter grasses
for tears might become icicles
hanging from eyeballs and lashes
for godsake let's go in and
drink mulled wine

it's may and we're standing
around the ultimate pit
young heads male and female bare
light breezes kissing our cheeks
lifting our uncoifed hair
except for the two passionate
friends of the body whose mourning
is expressed with shaved skulls
their hands are clasped
trying not to scratch the itch
of recovering follicles

but the mother's black straw
with white feathers
suggests the rattle
of a bygone hearse the stamp
of impatient black horses
tossing their noble heads
plumed out there
on the freshly gravelled road

After a Fire on the Cutting – 1959

One day, from a ditch by the tracks, I pick a stone heart out of the mud. It is white as marble with blurred bumps of purple showing where the valves could be, and at the apex a suggestion of cut-off stumps of vein and artery where the blood enters and pumps out into a body of dirty water.

Later scrambling up the bank I encounter evil in the guise of a burnt-out cloud of smoke – should a cloud have cinder eyes or a pair of muscular hands horny as claws to grasp me? And who knows what strange dominance could lead to a journey on another train of thought to the depot of the abandoned mind?

Nothing remains of the pebble but a ragged hole in the pocket of the stiff jeans I'm wearing as I climb among the charred stumps of trees asking will these lampblack smudges stay always with me though I scrub and scrub my wrists against rough denim thighs?

A Rescue

You bounce my shoulders suddenly out between one
wave and the next. "Chin up, chin up," you shout
over the roar of the deep and the crash of foam,
"for chrissake keep your nose above water."

Now we feel something slip between us, slide away
between our thighs. Could have been a gob of blood
perhaps or a twisting eel or a child, present or
past, getting shut of us making for blue water.

By this time I'm sick of your strength and the
show-off way you swim this stroke and that like a
champion from Australia. I kick you as hard as I
can and if our legs weren't in such a tangle
I could have floated off and followed our
putative daughter

to where on the far shore of the ocean she hauls
up on foreign rocks imagining herself the first
creature to leave this shifting element and try
her luck in the sandy heat of the sun.

Yggdrasil

in this city, the capital of winter, icetowers
grow like glass fungus from the snowy ground.

by February some have come to their zenith,
others are nubbled stubs will never reach
their full height,

for who can foretell the day of the melt when all
this will become so many pools of dirty water.

each tower has its hidden tenant,
one a bear, one a snake

one a squirrel, one a salamander
one a scarce prairie dog.

some like mine, like yours are home
to the daughters and sons of summer

we who have refused the bleak
hospitality of a winter outdoors

it's not that we are without faith
for we do believe that one of these turrets

holds safe the idea
of the tree of creation,

how it springs every year from a new seed
small as an apple pip,

how it suddenly splits
the imprisoning tower of cold

and, sooner than the sun expects,
buds and blossoms with flowers

pink as cradled babies swinging
from its green and pithy branches

Four Mile House

1. if I sit here long enough I'll hear and I'll
see the evening train rush by between my
brother's garden and the sky

2. steam and smoke cannot blacken the rooftiles of
his house which has always belonged to any of the
twenty-nine generations of his belonging in this
place

3. one day thieves let down a crane and caught up
his marble Daphne from her place on the high bank
of stones and lilies

4. one day a cloud descended and smothered his
beloved as she lay in their green-painted iron
bed with the red-lacquered heart at its head

5. one day his Australian swan froze into the ice
of the pond he waded in to rescue it and ruined
his trousers the swan died anyway his black and
white and red-billed companion

6. now arm in arm we circle the grey-flagged paths
not singing not speaking of the night we walked
all those miles home in the dark after the
theatre when our train was bombed

Assortment

some of those says the child
handing over her pocket money

pointing to the jar of many-coloured
sugared almonds

and could she please have one of each kind
all folded into a blue paper cone

but then how to give up those colours
just to make sugar to crunch nuts

her teeth white as kernels
her tongue pink as a bud

her greed dark as licorice
her avarice grey as fields
before they quicken into spring

She Steps Out

into the garden of the world
where there's a war every day

between plants and beetles
between beetles and birds

who dip their beaks once twice
three times into the water fountain
before setting out on the hunt

at night come the bats some swooping
over the flowerbeds seeking
for nocturnal flies and grubs

some to stick their tongues into night
blossoms pale in the moonlight

a cloud crosses the moon
darkness in the mind
murder amongst the leaves

and the crack of seedpods
that feeds the idea of life

abiding in a tiny mouthful
of sharp teeth

in small piles of green shit
fallen to the duff
of a forest to come

O Greenest Bough

(from the Latin of Hildegard von Bingen)

Aha, you greenest bough
lifted up into the forest air
on our thoughts and prayers

the hour has come
that every one of your twigs
shall blossom and we salute you
because it's from you
that the sun's warmth has come forth
as the scent exudes from the gum tree

it's from you that glorious flowers spring
scenting the desert air

when dew falls on the grass from the sky
they spread out their fresh petals
and the whole earth rejoices because
seed will come of it
and this is why the birds
have built their nests in your branches

when the fruit is ripe
there will be a great feasting
aha young woman
then the fullness of joy will be yours

can it be true that Eve cared nothing
for all these gifts of God?
O young woman, let us give thanks
let our praises rise to the heavens

Statement for *A Matter Of Spirit*

I read in a book: "Is not every child that dies a natural death slain by an Angel?" Aha Mr. Blake, does that explain the sunrise angels sitting on the sill of the East window each finger of their folded hands a fiercely burning flame? Is death by angel something to be desired?

I wander in the woods alone. I sit under a tall pine, the needle duff scratching my eight-year-old bum. The entity that is everything leans down explaining the universe, the oneness the separateness. I understand how, though we are apart, yet we are one. I understand at once this truth, this whole truth. But by the time I reach home I have forgotten how this works. I can't hold it. It has flown away like a careless bird. Day has ended. The dark night of the soul.

Much later I realize that though we are other from the divine we are sitting in the same chair. This is funny. This is bitter. This is absurd.

Then it is to the absurd, the tragic, the extremely funny I must turn to express that ordinary life beyond logic, beyond time.

And here I am trying to plant that tree once more, trying to build that house again, the one with the angels sitting on the sill of the East window. The sun rises behind their bowed heads. They lean down and write with the fire of their fingers. They may be themselves, they may be myself. I can only copy their words.

Part Two: Light from Light

The Russia of the Mind

In the Russia of the mind we are caught up in long
conversations which have great significance but little point.
"Life is fleeting," we tell each other, "in fact it has all been
over for several years now."

Before the end occurs we spend the summer at the dacha,
where the grass and the afternoons are longer than the life
of man.

All of this and much more we discuss one whole night round
a samovar: we wrap towels around our sweating heads and
converse with great seriousness until dawn.

Just as the rising sun lightens the waters of the great river,
we notice an old woman travelling on a huge dark barge. She
knows everything there is to know about life and a death
crueller than the sword. She sits upon a sack of grain all
dressed in black with her rough hands folded upon her lap.
Her eyes are on the river slowly streaming in the wake of the
craft. Surely one of us is a poet who will praise her endurance?

"Ah how difficult it is," she mutters under her breath, "to live
in the Russia of the mind — so different from the movies
where you have landscape music to carry you along."

Hadrian's Dream

no one can own his dreams H admits weeping
searching through river mud for the body of his beloved

those lily-stem legs those apple cheeks
those curls like the buds of primulas

and can he claim these tears now
they are part of the river rushing on

carrying the boy to the sea and beyond the sea
casting him up sprawled on the sand of the far shore

there a gang of maidens finds him and they weave
a litter of kelp and singing carry him
up to the house of his god

as for the emperor is this dream his house
this mourning his dwelling

did he buy it with the sweat
that stands out on his forehead as he sleeps

for can a man throw down handfuls of coins
to buy visions in some sort of market place

this market where all sorts of fruits and vegetables
are displayed in the open air under the staring sun

they're going bad and rotting apples attract wasps
who buzz about their business sipping

devouring those beginnings those cores full of seeds
that have become no more than discarded endings

and at the core this heart of things lies
his unattained ambition to own a small

but well-thought-of restaurant cooking
being the third arrow in the quiver of his desire

or should he just be content to call himself
the chef of the establishment

his reputation having gone before him
to the four corners of the district

from this reverie he looks up and smiles
and says well this is just a hole-in-the-wall

but no because how can a wall have holes when it's
quite tumbled down and its stones have for centuries
been carted off to make sheep pens

and this is the imperial wall of course
his wall to keep out and keep in

but like his love it must give way broken
in the end when at last the youth

steps into the water refusing to swim
his sweet destiny crushed
like apples in a cider press

You and I at the Rapids

1. Look, look, you say, this is the last of the river, it's broken and the pieces have tumbled into the lake.

2. I try to explain that the consolation of the eyes is nothing much, what they don't see being more evident than what they do, the flume of the cataract tossing everything to spray until the spume clouds my vision of the lakewater.

3. When I look down at my feet I see two curled snails sprinkled with waterdrops, when I look up a ship caught in the boughs of a winter tree like the moon on a postcard.

4. A storm comes up and the sails of the ship flip flap in the wind. The captain gives orders to down the mast. In the dark of the tempest I perceive his mouth moving, his chest heaving, but because of the howl of the wind I hear nothing but his cries.

5. Is this the hurricane of the mind which breaks light from light from light and becomes darkness?

6. As soon as I'm sure that you see what I see I'll close my eyes, my lashes resting tiredly on my cheeks like roots of old trees on the floor of the forest.

7. Now you, whose boast is clear-thinking clear-seeing, explain if you can, when this is fresh water, why salt burns my face and crusts on my lips and my tongue.

Dried Fruits and Herbs – An Autumn Basket

as soon as you show any interest in his subject,
he subjects you to a diatribe on his ideas.

idea is something he can't be objective about
for it is after all the object of his desire.

for an old scholar is like a dried fruit rattling
away hoping the whole thing will split open

and one seed at least will fall into a moisty mind
less dusty than his own,

still green and red-cheeked, but bitter
as any gall he says

ah gall home of wasp grub
ah robin's pincushion

now wasp emerges and how she buzzes
light lights upon her as she unfolds her wings
and wings her way after carrion after prey

thence to the petiole the stem the leaf
the rose arising as her idea

the sage the pome the wasp all gone
within one summer

Untitled ("This is not a trick ...")

This is not a trick, you say turning your hands palm up
and the palms are flowering with primulas, the pink branched kind
you can find in the woods at a certain time in the spring –
it's October now, snow threatening and you out here by the lake
without your gloves, and your hands flowering

What else can you do, what other falderals do you keep
up your sleeve – new green leaves and mudfish spawning,
a papery butterfly and the first crow calling

I came here to listen to the fierce crash of ice
I came to welcome whatever winter might bring
but you with a sparrow nesting in your hat
dancing and dancing on the frozen path
almost persuade me that this must be spring

Rowan in May

an eggshell is a house to be broken out of
a house is a shell to be broken into

I at the window, the bird in the tree
whose leaves are marbled with birdshit

my children roll dibs on the sidewalk
and I at my work already

painting a hex on my door
to warn away thieves

climbing the neighbour's fence
to thieve flowers for my table

on my table a loaf, a long knife
a cup a spoon and an apple

the children complain
what no butter, no jam?

afternoon and the sun has browned the edges
of the tree's white blossoms

later a small storm greys the sky

nightfall and now it's snowing
on the bird on her nest in the tree

Untitled ("The cowman ...")

The cowman is walking over the fields to work. He usually goes up the footpath, but this particular morning is so pearly and promising that he wants only to feel his feet on the springy turf, only to watch the sun rise between the distant pollarded willows with their spiky arms pointing upwards as though in salutation to the day.

When he comes to the water-meadow he will, unless he wants to get his boots wet, have to skirt along the ditch where the iron-red water is running under a hedge of briar and honeysuckle. He's a tall man and the briars catch in his hair and the withies slap his cheeks as he goes. But the morning is so hopeful and the man so young and full of himself that these small itches worry him not at all.

Not that he is without worries. As a matter of fact it's always irked him that somehow his mouth is not made for whistling and that, however much he licks his lips and puckers his mouth, the only sound that comes out is a low flat moaning like the winter wind in the chimney, and what good is that to a young fellow bent on expressing his satisfaction with the strength of his limbs and the lightness of his handsome head?

But at least he can sing and he does, the same line over and over from a song he once heard. He's not musical and his voice is growly and flat, but anyway he can belt out the words:

> *My love is afoot in the forest*
> *And her feet are like swords in my heart*

But how can feet be like swords? He could change that to stars – her feet are like stars in my heart. Or flowers her feet are like ... But you could go on like that forever. Swords, stars, flowers. How about leaves or tears? Or loaves of bread, or jars of jam, or for that matter reflections, conclusions, disbeliefs.

Well that's it, disbelief. That's the cloud that follows him
everywhere. Just above his head. Raining on his head no matter
how bright the day everywhere else. The rain of disbelief pelts
down, not that it actually wets his hair but yet he can feel it
always pelting, pelting, each drop hitting hard like a truth that he
can't bring himself to admit.

By now he's crossed the field and entered the spinney. A poor
excuse for a forest he thinks it. But trees are trees and you could
imagine the virgin forest that once covered the land from one sea
to the other. At least he has heard that there is a sea to the west.
A rocky shore and dashing waves. He has a cousin who claims to
have once walked that way and found that shore. Not sandy at all,
he had said, just rocks and rocks and the sea dashing in like an
angry evil child.

And it's that he's afraid of. The child that dances always before
him on the grass, between the trees, in and out the ruined
buildings that he passes on the moor. Milking cows or tending
pastures. Is this the evil child who laughs at him from his heart
or his hand. Is this the one?

Untitled ("In the park he tosses ...")

In the park he tosses a ball into the air, hears his mother calling him in from play. It's raining, raining, raining, she cries, you'll catch cold, your death out there.

He runs in through the usual yellow-painted door, which closes behind him with the usual firm click. But when his eyes get used to the dim he sees that the house is quite other, with passages and staircases he has never known. Up and down the stairs he runs in and out the many rooms, opening and closing the closets, kicking the baseboards. There's nothing else to kick. No tables no chairs no beds no chests, but the empty walls are papered with curious hunting scenes and parrots in forest trees and climbing plants with flowers as stiff as biscuits.

In the basement there is nothing at all but a grand piano resting on the concrete floor. It is open with music ready to play a song with words that will not come to his tongue, though in his mind he remembers them.

In the attic a girl sits on the window seat gazing out the dormer window into a cool pearly mist like the fog that comes up from the sea. The girl's hair is pale and split at the ends like his imaginings, like his many questions. Her neck moves from side to side waving as gently as the stem of a crinoid, a sea lily. The boy longs to look into her eyes. He imagines them hazel or amber. He imagines them grey with green flecks like floating algae. But he knows he must leave before she can turn and recognize him, before she can turn and claim him.

Standing sturdily on the grass of the park he catches the ball as it plummets, while a few thick drops of rain begin to trickle down his face like tears.

A Child and his Mother Camp Out
  on a Cool Night

The child putting his hands together thinks his prayer is
like a pancake his mother has baked for him. She poured
batter on a hot stone and when the edges curled she
folded it and placed it between his fingers. And the
pancake is a flower folded at sunset, and the flower is a
nest hidden in a tree and the nest hung there in the sky is
a dark star.

If you want light, his mother tells him, you must pray for
it. Shine this flashlight to your ear and it will brighten the
inside of your skull. You'll see light through to the forests
of the mind, where birds sleep all night in their nests in
the trees and stars hang down from the branches like
icicles.

Precursing

on the day I entered this world
no one came to greet me
only my mother knew that I had been born
for her dark tunnel felt so empty

she lay on her bed in the afternoon
listening to the rain on the windows
predicting her next child
    he should have a head like a broad boulder of jade
    he should have silver feet with little wings at the heel
    he should have a golden torso like a picture she had seen
    in a health magazine while she was lying in

she thought of him constantly
while I lay by her side
wailing into the new air
"it was a sunday" she told me years later
"a lucky day to be born"

but that was a lie for I remember
that the shops were open
people walked up and down the wet street
outside and neon lights refracted from puddles
flickered over my face
should I ever get out of my pinned
flannel binder I wondered
and find my feet
and splash about on the wet pavement?

after a long time my mother
put out her grudging hand to touch my head
her fingertip moved coolly along the curve of my cheek
I tried to catch it in my mouth for I wanted
to suck on it and feel the difference
between her soft flesh and the sharp polished nail

as she lifted me to her she thought again
about my brother who should come after me
    how he would have hair like a black wing
    how his face would glow with sunlight
    how his shoulders would be straight and warm

"he will press my full breast between his fisted hands"
she murmured "he will suck so hard I will have to cry out
and later when his teeth have sprouted
he will grind the nipple between them
and draw blood"

Statement: Reinventing Memory

Reinventing memory can only, like Jacob's ladder, be an idea.
How many steps to Heaven? How many steps to the reinvention
of memory? First there is experience, then memory, then the
invention of that memory, and, after all that, the reinvention?

Memory may be, in our minds, the only proof of the existence
of linear time. So and so many years ago this and this happened.
I can count the days, the months, the years. I can remember the
face of my mother, her long coil of red hair. The scratch of the
pips on the khaki shoulder of my father as he embraces me. Is
this memory? Is this invention? Yes, first I must invent memory,
but I don't want to see my memories as inventions, to me these
are facts, something existing still in the past of linear time.

I look back in space as well as time. I see myself as a child
sleeping under a tree, as a lost child wandering the roads at
night. I'm sleepwalking into the village in my skimpy white
nightdress. I'm squatting outside a lighted shop window, peeing
on the warm pavement. Open your eyes, child; it's only a
memory an invented life a narrative of dreams.

I remember, I remember the house where I was born. But that's
impossible, my father tells me. I must have made up that house.
It was a flat, my father tells me, in a dusty part of London. But it
rained when you were born. It laid the dust. It made the dust
into the thinnest layer of mud over everything. Yes, yes, I answer.
I remember that.

Mother's white and freckled breast, milk flowing into the
corners of my mouth, rain pittering on the hood of my pram;
I do remember these I do. And because of my memories, the
whole Universe has been changed forever.

Another story: Once I bore a daughter, I wrapped her in the
blanket of my past. This child inherits all my memories. Have I

invented her, my daughter? She remembers my childhood as her own, her grandmother's childhood as though it might be a bedtime story. Is seeing backwards, seeing into the past, simply a memory? Do we invent the memories of our foremothers?

And can we remember the future? For I see her shutting her eyes for the last time. Her wispy locks spread out upon a pillow of dark velvet. She's dead, her hair the last thing living of her. Her daughter, long-legged in her wry middle age, leans over and snips at her hair wiry and iron-grey. She grasps the lock, unlocks the door, throws the grey skein to the prairie wind. The hair unravels and unravels; threads catch on the grass, threads wind on the twigs of low shrubs. Who will knit up these strands of thought and power into a web of memory?

The bones of women are piled up behind the door. The skulls speak and are answered by the songs of children. Is this the invention of memory – the reinvention?

Part Three: Day of Wings

Fear of Knives

The young woman stands by the window holding something up to the light. It could be a feather from the wing of a dove. It could be the leaf of that lily plant whose blossom heavy with scent bends almost to the earth, something she could certainly see through the clear pane if she stood on a chair and looked out.

If the light should fall on this thing, she believes, it will either melt into itself or into the idea of itself, a dagger, that is, a kris, a bright blade.

Soon twilight will fill every part of the room. It will creep out from the corners hiding the pattern on the wallpaper, which is parrots in a tropical forest, hiding the dusty squares where pictures once hung in their frames, in their glory.

She imagines the paintings as battle scenes with horses and chariots and flashing swords, or perhaps the smaller ones were simply illustrations torn from the Book of Weapons, badly framed and hung slightly askew. Why, she asks, did no one bother to straighten them?

Once, in another house, when they were children, her brother was given a skinning knife for Christmas. She remembers how envy filled up her mind like sour cranberry juice in a cup. She had plotted to somehow wrest that knife from him, but all day he kept it buttoned in the pocket of his jerkin, safe in its sheath.

At night it lay under his pillow with his other treasures, a white stone with a hole in it big enough for a little finger to poke through, a worn Clovis point he had found one day on the pathway to school. These things were of no interest to his sister whose one desire was the blade with the elk-horn handle.

Dark falls at last, and the woman remembers both her desire and her fear. How, if she managed to thrust her hand under the pillow and steal away the knife, she had planned to bury it in a hole in the garden. How she had planned to tell herself as she covered the sharp curve of the blade with damp earth that she was hiding her brother in a place where no one would ever find him again.

Untitled ("when earth leaps up ...")

when earth leaps up
and heaven descends
and the two meet like lovers
then the question is
could these flowers be stars

and is dust nothing
more than the handful
I sprinkled on your face
as you went down into the dirt

by now I suppose you've crumbled
and your best jacket eaten
by creatures smaller than sandgrains
by creatures so tiny that sandgrains
are their planets this fistful
of earth their universe

they hold hands like children
circling and singing in a playground
you hear them and your elegant bones
turn in the box and as you clap
the carpals of your wrists
fall away from each other

how simple the words to their song
all about blossoming stars
you can join in if you want to

here above ground
all I have left is the question

Untitled ("When I think of him ...")

When I think of him I say
"He is lost to me."
I should say perhaps
"He is found to himself."
For his is now that ample
silence he wanted in a woman.

At last he is safe from my demand
that he answer, that he speak.
Safe from my shrieking dancing
and tears, from my challenging
him with a thick branch of words.

Once I beat upon a pot
for an hour with a metal spoon
simply to save him
from his own grim silence
which I thought then
to be worse than death.

Now I know that for the living
there is nothing worse than death.

Untitled ("long ago you imagined …")

long ago you imagined your sinews
as that toughest kind of wire
twisted of many strands
and when a tree fell you thought
that you had toppled it
with a touch of your finger
that it pitched down a mountainside
that you raced after it, and hardly
breaking your stride carried it off
and planted it by a parched river
somewhere south of winnipeg

and had I known you then
swaggering over the hills
crushing the stones into sand
would I understand your face
how it is like the face
of a regular army major
whose thin-lipped smile
made him a whip over africa

now in your whisky-husky voice
you explain that the sparks of your
steel-tipped boots over flint
were a boy's trick any girl
could be shown and not believe in

will you ever dare to tell
your fear of the dull year's turning
how it softens the stony grasp
how it rusts and notches
the violent edge

Lullaby For Mark

When they rocked my cradle
I could hear the swinging
of the nearby sea
how it sucked at the shore
swallowing soft animals
tough wrack hard shells
spitting them up half eaten
along the tideline

as I close you in my arms
the wind rocks the fields
it shakes the grass into rivers
which pound at our barred door
sleep now against my sleeping shoulder
may each of us awaken in his own place

yours shall be an island
heavy with white sand
where gaunt shaggy ponies
nibble the spikegrass
where in april seals heave up
to bear their spotted young

mine shall be a glacial lake
fenced by the forest
under its lid of ice
broken spears lie drowned
bones of dark fishermen
pebbles that were arrows
anchors that are stones

Kakky Poem Three

however old you get
I know that I will be
even older   my confident
step goes before your
tentative one   I encourage
you up ladders and trees
when you tumble I brush
the crumbled bark from
your knees and explain
how I can't understand your
fear of heights, your
fear of falling
      branches and towers
are nothing to me I say
even the mountains
feel flat beneath my feet

and now we are here at the peak
there's something more I can
teach you   look, every day
since the beginning I have flown
in the cold glint of air
every morning I've taken off
bobbing under the clouds

I touch my fingertips
to yours they are joined

Mother and Daughter Dancing in a Garden

Sundown. The housedoor closed. Two women dancing in the garden. Dark footsteps on pale grass. Crushed flowers in the border. Heel holes at the very edge of things.

This is an unexpected visit, the young one says, not quite out of breath. She's rejoicing but all the same not exactly pleased.

We're just lucky this time, Grey replies somewhat grimly, kicking her heels even higher. She's showing off of course, her right foot almost touching the other's shoulder. Take care, says the daughter, leaning back, demurring, any minute now you could ruin my makeup.

But their laughter dissolves all that, and up they jump, their toes twinkling as they cast off their shoes, careless as the wind that cools their faces. Their words fly round and round like music while their attitudes exaggerate themselves in the dusk. And when at last the hour brings darkness, anyone would say these two must surely have exhausted the possibilities of such a relationship, but that's not how it ends.

Now whether it has something to do with the conversation, a question unanswered, an idea not explained, or whether it's the last line of a half-remembered lyric that will not come to mind, suddenly that's all there is to it.

Someone has locked the door from the inside. No access. And the women are stopped there in their flight, the one with her mouth pressed forever to the other's ear.

Grief

I shall rise only to make coffee or sandwiches or to visit the bathroom. Even this I shall do reluctantly: by march I shall hardly be able to move from my chair to my bed, from my bed to my chair.

Then one day spring will appear again with its flurry of digging and seeding, and I shall forget that I ever said this or did it. Thus will my life wear on from season to season from equinox to equinox, until one spring I shall find myself unable to get up from my chair, my book, my melancholy. I shall be left gazing through the window at my daughter, herself by this time grown into a stout grandmother, or at least a great aunt, walking barefoot between the rows of the garden, a measure of carrot seed held lightly in her palm. From time to time she will rest from her continual bending and flinging and stare up at the lead blue of the sky which threatens, or perhaps promises, rain.

To a Friend Dying

these last days
how changeable you are
one moment an old woman
shining and crumpled
as a spring leaf

the next a busty girl
lovers out on the street
can hear you calling them
to your bed

for your comfort
I bring a saltglazed pot
with thornbranch growing
blossoms still furled
in the spiked stem's black nipples

and I tell you the sermon
I shall give at your funeral
"this is only the beginning
of change" I shall say
as I bury your pupa
into its mound of dirt

"on the day of wings
something shall certainly emerge
perhaps not flesh
perhaps not what you expect"

Untitled ("it's morning ...")

it's morning and you bring me the skull
of a mouse white as paper

at noon you hand me the jaw of a pony
brown as milk chocolate

well I just need a few more bones
to build myself a lover

go find me a lizard pelvis
narrow as a mountain pass

beef shoulders too
broad as any harbour

and I'll have to have ribs of course
and little foot bones
and the ivory curve of a rattler's spine

by evening light we'll work
intricately wiring this piece to that

and then at last lie down
all three knotted in the moonlight

Statement on Peace

And what is this thing called peace? You may come upon it suddenly in the garden or the forest. It is a whole thing, indivisible.

Pax, says the priest, *vobiscum.* Now if only that dove could fly easily from head to head, from one's mouth to another's ear, but that journey is so hard and long. The frail little thing can so easily be shot down as it wings its way to nest in understanding.

Pax, says the child, crossing her fingers. What she means is *truce, truce; let me get my breath long enough to begin the fight all over again.*

Is everything then simply a balance of violences with peace at the heart like the silence at the heart of a storm?

We cannot see the borders of the universe, which way it bends to come back to us. For the edges are amorphous and changing, and space hanging over the belt of stars like too much flesh on a man.

But the biosphere in our eyes is rounded and whole and self-contained as a garden in a bottle. Or it's a soap bubble with everything contained within its delicate iridescent skin.

My drawings, my poems I think of as bubbles of quiet, each one perfect as it comes from the clay pipe but falling quickly in my estimation until there seems nothing for it but to blow another.

Grant us Thy peace. But only the peace of infant sleep, which any moment may turn to shrieks angry enough to awaken the quick and the dead.

Part Four: The Great Crocodile

Taxonomy

in the sky a dwarf whiter than any milk on earth
giants roam the middle distance   the sun fails and
falls into our usual dream, the one about the
condition of our existence

in the bed between lovers' limbs vines creep
bearing flowers that are trumpets   their sound is
like the odours of pollination   are they rejoicing
that the names of their nations have been written
down?

nothing can change the order of things written thus
scribes attempt to circumscribe our lives and the
bodies roll over on the mattress and the mattress
kisses the double leaves that so much resemble lips

all of this under a canopy which could mean a
marriage or simply that the garden is too hot this
time of year

one more time   lie down dear one she says and
into your mind my words will creep like toffee-
coloured creatures trembling as they enter your ears
the centre of flowers their buds and anthers
responding to the six-footed tread heavy as an army
of ancient spearsmen marching through coiled
passages carrying their weapons half-concealed
under their cloaks

and already as they journey they repeat their names
their ranks and numbers setting all this to a military
air   we who hear their familiar words follow on,
follow like clever rats like foolish gods making
conversation

singing phon and antiphon into the dark

A Catechism (or Conversation)
Phon and Antiphon

Ph. It's true, isn't it, that to return to God is to come back to oneself?

A. Self, self, what self is that?

Ph. The endowment, the name, speech and seeds. You could call it voice.

A. Who gave you this voice?

Ph. I was given it in the beginning. I was born blind as a kitten and could not see the face of the great Donor.

A. Were you deaf, too? Tell me about His voice.

Ph. I can tell you this much – there was no indication that the Donor is male.

A. Female then?

Ph. Not particularly.

A. A child then?

Ph. Not particularly.

A. A Crocodile?

Ph. Possibly.

A. So what did the Great Crocodile say? I suppose you can at least remember that?

Ph. Difficult. The Voice was kind of growly.

A. Aha, I thought so, a male crocodile.

Ph. You think female crocodiles have soprano voices? Are there operas, then, on the banks of the Nile?

A. Aida.

Ph. So God spoke – sang – to me in Italian you think?

A. Perhaps that's the reason ...

Ph. ... for what?

A. For how hard to understand those words were.

Ph. I tried my very best, but ... how about you? Did you understand those first words?

A. How could I, I who was born deaf as a bat?

Ph. Bats aren't deaf.

A. How do you know?

Ph. I read it in a book.

A. What book? Anyway, you said you were born blind.

Ph. I got my sight when my mother took me to the Holy Spring.

A. Did she dip you in?

Ph. I'll say. The water was fucking cold.

A. *(piously)* We're in the sight, hearing of the Sacred Reptile, who may not want to be subjected to your vulgarities.

Ph. In the sight of God all words are holy. It says so in the Bible.

A. The f-word isn't in the Bible.

Ph. It's in the Anglo-Saxon Bible.

A. So now God is an Anglo-Saxon crocodile?

Ph. There's no evidence to the contrary.

A. There are no crocodiles in the Thames.

Ph. Not now, but there used to be. Teeth have been found, and the remnants of a scaly tail.

A. A likely tale.

Ph. As likely as any other. As likely as our existence.

A. Or our persistence, these centuries.

Ph. These many years.

A. These days.

Ph. These long moments.

A. Glitches.

Ph. Hitches.

A. To the trousers of time.

A Herring Lives in the Sea

He's pretty sure it's the sea, though after all there are such creatures as freshwater herrings. All he can see is the clear green water above, and beneath him the murky sand, and of course the tails of the fishes that swim before him in his particular school.

It is his joy and despair to live out his life among so many of his fellows, for what could be more exciting than the swoosh of synchronized movement as the whole group dashes in and out of drowned wrecks and kelp forests like a silvery sinuous breeze?

Not that everything is certain for a herring. This one swims always in the centre of the school and therefore cannot make out whether he is following those in front or being chased by those behind. Both, perhaps.

A fish swimming in a school has the fortune, or the misfortune, to be at the same time a completely social animal and a completely solitary one. This at least gives him the opportunity for conjecture and speculation while he is exercising his shining body and delicate fins. It is like being a hermit, he decides, and at the same time a not unimportant member of a tight community. The fish consoles himself with the knowledge that some monasteries, both Christian and Buddhist, work on the same principle.

Nevertheless any creature may sometimes stray, and one day, for one reason or another, the herring lags behind his fellows and drops out of the stream of things for just a moment. The school happens to be passing over a reef at the time, and a large grouper darts out of its lair and snaps him up in one gulp.

And so the herring has left one entity to become part of another, part of a large and very solitary fish with a huge mouth and a wide lazy body. The grouper lurks all day and night under its stony shelf, waiting for unwary creatures to stray from their appointed places. Snap go its toothy jaws as it swallows this one and that one into its roomy stomach. The herring – who is now assimilated into the grouper – can't help being somewhat amused at his fate. Now he has become a solitary creature who is yet an integral part of the reef on which he lives and on which he depends. Does nothing ever really change for any of God's creatures? It is a wonder, he thinks, that the Almighty hasn't bored Himself out of existence long ago.

A Green Hill

For practice the hunter fastens
an old straw hat to a post.

His keen eye stares at this target
between the sights of his rifle,
along the shaft of his arrow.

His prey speaks: *wait*
she says *remember how it used to be*
when I was nailed to my door
and you to your tree

when I was a horseshoe
and you a dead crow

when I was a hex
and you a crooked board

when I was an edict
and you a king's title

The hunter levels his weapon

wait she says *first we should drink*
first we should dance
first we should mourn the pity of it
how a young man's feet so sprightly prance
under the gallows tree
take my hand dance with me

but the shell's in the barrel
the arrow's in the groove
no one can wait on memory
still less on love

the hunter levels his weapon
the hunter draws his bow
the hat falls an empty thought
to the wet grass below

Untitled ("How strange it is ...")

"How strange it is," I remark to a cat sitting in a basket chair, "that you and I should live together day after day without flying off the handle. It's true that you take advantage of me at every turn, but then how cosy you keep my feet of a winter's night: how sweetly you purr before the fire."

The cat flicks its ears, disdainful of my human weakness that leads to these endless strings of spoken words.

Presently I sit down in the opposite chair and doze in the warmth of the sunporch. As I nod off, the cat's unblinking eyes are the last things I see. They grow huge and green confusing my dreams.

Each eye is a whole world: they have become separate planets revolving in the dark of the cat's fur. Or rather one of them is the moon of the other. It is impossible to guess which.

The Winter Cat

I don't agree, says the cat, shifting its position a little on the old woman's foot, I don't agree at all.

That, says the woman, plying her needle between the three layers of cloth in the square she is patching, is because you're a cat. It's different for a woman. Quite different.

Different how? and the cat looks up rather belligerently into the woman's eyes. For once she has looked at the cat, has lifted her eyes from her work. The pattern, if you looked at it one way, was called Tumbling Blocks, if another way Eastern Star, the colours grey and ivory and a surprising shade of burnt orange – and any prints she's been able to find that complement these colours, in fact, are almost the colours of the cat's abundant coat. She certainly has an eye for the garish, the cat muses, turning its face away in the direction of the window. Different how?

The woman has come to a difficult turn in the pattern and doesn't answer right away. The March evening is drawing in and it's time to light the lamp. Either that or she can put her work aside for a few minutes and try to answer the cat's impertinent question.

It's like this, she wants to say. It's like that. But how could a cat understand? It has something to do with, well, love.

The cat makes no attempt to hide its scorn for such a ridiculous answer. If a cat could manage a sceptical smile, it would. As it is it manages to convey a very proper sneer.

The woman foolishly tries to mend matters by going into more and more details – the arm round the shoulders, the hand lightly stroking the breast. The words *I love you, I love you,* the faces getting closer, the lips touching, the kiss, the ...

But the cat has heard enough already and gets up and stalks across the room, leaps on a chair by the window, pricks up its ears and watches for a few minutes with great attention the shadowy world of the garden and the pathway beyond. The world of night hunting, and of dark rumours, and of course the world of feline sexual encounters. The cat, who is entering its heat, is beginning to feel uneasy and excited, and oh that terrible longing, that inconsolable desire for another wilder life where stealth and cunning are everything.

Beyond the garden and the dirt pathway there is the Wood, a dense thicket of trees and undergrowth just now quickening into spring. A yellowish haze of new leaves clouds the branches of the oaks and elms, and the sallows and willows are putting out their upright silvery catkins. It's there that the cat spends its summers. Relishing its freedom. Giving birth to a litter of kittens in the underbrush. And hunting, always hunting, mouse tail and bird wing littering the forest floor around its den. Can there be any more exciting life than that one? In summer the cat forgets the woman who feeds and shelters its winters, who sits and sews and chats by the yellow light of the lamp, who walks out to the gate to pick up the can of milk that the farmer leaves there every morning. Who shares her life and food with the cat. In summer the cat is the Wild Cat of the Woods and that is that.

You might well think that the opposite is true – that in winter the cat is entirely engrossed in its domestic life in the cosy warmth of the house. But that's not quite so, as it sits there enjoying the lamplight and the firelight and the dinner that the woman puts down in the dish marked, absurdly, CAT in blue on the china rim. (How can a cat be expected to read – even a cat who can hold a conversation as well as this one?)

The woman, who is a good deal sharper than the cat imagines, knows very well that her winter companion dreams always of its summer self. Never far from the animal's mind is that other, the hunter, the stalker, the accurate triumphant pouncer.

But there is always another side to every question, every speculation and desire. What does the cat care about the woman's thoughts, for instance? How they go back to her lively youth of assignations and trysts. How she wonders about her lost children, her faint-hearted suitors, her ardent but faithless lovers whose faces appear in her dreams, whose deceitful words echo in her ears still.

One day in early autumn, when the weather is getting cooler and damper, and prey is getting scarcer and more wary, the cat, who is after all a practical creature, decides the time has come to leave its wild existence and take up residence once more in the cottage by the edge of the woods.

When it brushes the front door as the first snow sprinkles the front step, when it jumps up against the door yowling softly and asking to be let in, how can the cat know that the woman for a moment imagines a tall man, bent now perhaps with age, standing there with a faded bouquet of autumn leaves in his hand, a gift for an old flame at last remembered, or perhaps a young woman with a half-remembered face, a shawl-wrapped child sleeping in her arms.

Of course, of course, it is just the usual winter cat. Come in,
come in, says the woman in a welcoming way, already her
mind going forward to some of the discussions, one might
almost call them arguments, she looks forward to having with
her friend, who stalks in as though it owns the place – the
house, the hearth, the cat dish, even the woman herself,
whom the cat imagines to have been longing all summer for
its scratch at the door, for its wet paws marking up the just-
washed, just-polished bluestones of the cottage floor.

A Conversation

God said: Above all, take care of your skin. Take notice of all
those commercials on TV, those double-spread ads in the
ladymags. Believe me those purveyors of unguents and creams
and lotions know what the hell they're talking about. I don't
want you returning to me when your time's up with
wrinkles and blotches, acne scars, things like that.

*What difference will it make? My skin, like the rest of me, will
either rot or burn. That's been your rule from way back at the
beginning, hasn't it?*

I, who made everything, also invented the metaphor. Please
keep the image of your skin as I first made it, smooth and
clear of blackheads and blemishes. At the end, I want to
receive you as I sent you out, enclosed in a perfect epidermis.

*By then I'll be a drudged-out old crone, bags under red eyes, sagged
at the chin, maybe a wen in my cheek. I'll sit all day at my
spinning, all night at my weaving by the light of a single candle,
flickering like my life.*

Flicker flicker flicker. Light soft as a baby's skin.

I'll be at work on my last project. A shroud of many colours.

Better you learn to knit. In knitting you can pick up one
strand and twist it with another. Here, let me show you how
a thread of matter may be caught up with a strand of image
so that they seem always to have been a part of one another.
Very much as you are a part of me.

I am?

A long sweater down to your knees. Isn't that better than a shroud?

It is a shroud. An eternal garment.

Like a skin

Or a woolly bag

It will cover you.

Warm and itchy.

Tell me what you imagine encloses the Ecosphere, or indeed the Universe? Daughter, there is a nightgown for everything.

Everything in its own covering forever?

Well, just until I can find a fool brave enough to stick out his forefinger and tear open the white envelope of time.

To Be a Pilgrim

A woman travelling in a far city is walking up the steps of a church. She has a brochure in her hand which explains the life of the saint who is buried in this very place, who was martyred here right at the top of this hill, the apex, the brochure explains, of holiness.

The woman thinks of the past, how this whole landscape was once nothing more than the bed of a great sea, how primitive sharks and coelacanths darted heavily about without a thought, except of course for their prey. Standing there amongst them she imagines a primrose butterfly fish swimming daintily between her legs.

Give the earth a few more years, she explains to herself, and once again the sea will rush in and crabs will scutter along these ledges happy to find a place to teach their young how to walk on slippery surfaces. But then she may have to discard this picture if she remembers that crabs are not maternal enough to teach their young anything, let alone how to dance the dance of future ages. She tries her best to recall everything she has ever read about these creatures, but nothing comes to mind. Nothing that is but that shuffling side to side, in and out.

Now she looks down at her feet, which are becoming tired from so much climbing, and yes they have acquired a definite sideways movement, crablike possibly. Never mind that; she struggles determinedly on. Up up she goes, but, however many steps she climbs, the house where the saint dwells gets no nearer. It still is small in the distance, grey and a little vague. True there is a choir singing, but the sound of those voices gets no louder, no louder than a musical whisper, a faint fluting. Yet she knows that up there far above, her children are carefully enunciating words in a language she once used every day and even now, after all these years, still has not quite forgotten.

Afterword
by Mark Abley

Anne Szumigalski was 77 years old when she died on Earth Day 1999, soon after a diagnosis of cancer. She made a real effort in her last months to organize her papers and computer files, assembling more than half the poems in this book into a preliminary manuscript. Even so, nobody could claim that the crammed folders in her small Saskatoon home were in the best of order. Like so many artists and writers, Anne did not place a huge value on tidiness. Besides which, she intended to go on living a while longer.

I had been Anne's friend since I was a boy – to dispel any misapprehension, though, I must note that the lullaby in this book, almost certainly its earliest poem, is addressed to her son Mark, not to me. As her literary executor, my prime task was to decide whether those overflowing folders contained enough good poems to justify a final volume. (She also left behind an incomplete novella and an unfinished play – but her first love, her morning star, was always poetry.) The call was easy to make. It wasn't just a question of Anne's reputation, which had grown steadily in her last years, particularly after she won a Governor General's Award for her 1995 collection *Voice*. More important was my sense that some, perhaps many of these poems are up to the standard of her best writing – or to put it another way, they happily join a body of poetic work that ranks with any created in Canada late in the 20th century.

But I need to come clean, and state that the book you are holding is not the book that Anne would have sent out for publication had she lived another year or two. The poems are by no means first drafts; yet had she lived, she would doubtless have made some final revisions. Apart from correcting a few obvious typos, I did not alter any of her words or play with her line breaks. The title is mine; she was not ready to name the collection, even on a provisional basis. I am also responsible for the poems' order, although luckily I had a couple of lists to work from (Anne being Anne, the lists don't agree with each other). *When Earth Leaps Up* remains, in a sense, perpetually a work in progress. Her "Poems" file on a crimson diskette held 22 pieces of work; this book includes all of them, and adds another 18.

These extra pieces come from a variety of sources. Two prose statements have appeared in anthologies, though not in any of Anne's own books. A few pieces formed part of two late, small volumes, *Fear of Knives* and *Sermons on Stones,* which were published by Hagios – a Saskatoon press that was, at the time, run by her friend John Livingstone Clark. Those books did not enjoy a wide distribution. My trickiest decisions had to do with the unpublished poems lying loose among her papers, both at home and in the University of Regina archives where Anne donated materials in 1991. Often these poems exist in several versions with varying titles (and no dates, alas). In such cases I've tried to choose the version that works best as a finished poem, but there's no guarantee Anne would have approved of my choices. She scribbled drafts of poems on anything that came to hand – a letter from the Writers' Union of Canada, a paper napkin, an ACTRA Fraternal Benefit Society envelope, a credit application to Canada Concrete ...

One of the poems I found in the Regina archives is the untitled, plainspoken piece beginning "When I think of him." I include it here with some trepidation. It's possible Anne would have been horrified to see the poem in print; almost certainly she wrote it after the death of her husband, Jan Szumigalski, in 1986. It has the heartfelt directness of a journal entry. But it's also a fine poem, one that fits the preoccupations of this volume; and, after all, Anne did not hide or destroy it.

When Earth Leaps Up is Anne Szumigalski's last collection of poetry. A final volume of her miscellaneous writing, however, should appear within the next few years. As well as prose, drama, liturgy and the text for a dance piece, it will contain some of the poems which, quietly, tentatively, she began to mail out as early as 1961 – poems that appeared in a few of the country's finest magazines, but which have never been collected in book form. I thought about including them here, then rejected the idea. They seem too different from her late work in terms of style, form and even imagery.

Like all her other books, this one mingles wildness and domesticity, death and transformation, high seriousness and subversive humour. But in contrast to most of her published work, *When Earth Leaps Up* has a kind of pared-down intensity. It was largely written in the autumn of Anne's life, yet the book is seldom autumnal. Poem after poem alludes to spring, the muddy season of pellmell rebirth. On many pages, Anne – previously such a celebrant of language – seems to be looking beyond words. Some of the ecstatic and undulating extravagance of her earlier style – "the beluga / white as a pontiff's garment," even the snowshoe hare "foraging all night / her colours made chalky by the moon / her wary eye on the shadow of an owl" – has been winnowed away to arrive at an idiom equally risky but rougher, less exalted.

"No one can wait on memory," she warns in the poem "A Green Hill." Yet now, years later, I recall the April day when Anne's friends and family gathered about her grave. Saskatoon was no longer the capital of winter; flowers were already quickening in her garden. A small storm laid the dust and greyed the sky. Salt burned our faces. Out of our sight, the stars blossomed. Yet all around us, the Woodlawn Cemetery was alive with snowshoe hares, mating and fighting among the newly dead, dancing on the recently frozen paths. Absurd and tragic? Maybe. But it was also extremely funny. And, as Anne reminds us, "this is only the beginning of change."

Acknowledgments

Many of these poems were first published in *Prairie Fire* and *Malahat Review.*

"After a Fire on the Cutting" first appeared in *Sermons on Stones* (Hagios Press, Saskatoon, 1997). "A Herring Lives in the Sea," "A Catechism (or Conversation)," "Fear of Knives" and "The Winter Cat" first appeared in *Fear of Knives* (Hagios Press, 2000). They are reprinted here by generous permission.

"Reinventing Memory" was published in the League of Canadian Poets' *Museletter* (1993) and in *Imprint and Casualties,* ed. Anne Burke (Broken Jaw Press, 2000). "Statement for *A Matter of Spirit*" appeared in *A Matter of Spirit: Recovery of the Sacred in Contemporary Canadian Poetry,* ed. Susan McCaslin (Ekstasis Press, 1998). Anne Szumigalski originally wrote "Statement on Peace" for an exhibition of her own drawings.

The editor is delighted to thank Hilary Clark for her preface and Elizabeth Philips for her valuable work on the manuscript. Thanks also to the staff of the Archives and Special Collections, University of Regina, which preserved several of these poems among their extensive Anne Szumigalski holdings.

Author Biography

Anne Szumigalski (née Davis) was born on January 3, 1922, in London, England. Her large family soon moved to a Hampshire village, where she began to write as a child. During the Second World War she worked as an interpreter, medical auxiliary and welfare officer for the British Red Cross, first in England, then on the continent. In 1946 she married a Polish émigré, Jan Szumigalski. They would have four children. After several years in north Wales, the family moved to Saskatchewan, living in the Big Muddy region near the U.S. border before settling permanently in Saskatoon in 1956.

Proud to identify herself as a "prairie poet," she played a huge role in the development of literary culture in Saskatchewan from the 1960s onward. She was a founding editor of *Grain,* a founding member of the Saskatchewan Writers Guild, a longtime teacher at the Saskatchewan Summer School of the Arts, and the first writer-in-residence at the Saskatoon Public Library. In 1990 she received a lifetime award for excellence in the arts from the Saskatchewan Arts Board, as well as a life membership in the League of Canadian Poets. Apart from these formal honours, she was a friend and mentor to dozens of writers, in Saskatoon and far beyond.

Anne Szumigalski's first book of poetry, *Woman Reading in Bath,* appeared in 1974. It would be followed by fourteen others, including the Governor General's Award-winning *Voice* in 1995 and a major volume of selected poetry, *On Glassy Wings,* in 1997. Both *Arc* and *Prairie Fire* devoted special issues to her work. She died in Saskatoon on April 22, 1999.

Editor Biography

Mark Abley was born in 1955 and grew up mostly in Alberta and Saskatchewan. In 1971 he joined the "Saskatoon Poetry Group," informally led by Anne Szumigalski. Her example and influence were crucial to his own development as a writer.

Abley is the author or editor of ten books, including the internationally acclaimed work of non-fiction *Spoken Here: Travels Among Threatened Languages.* A former journalist with the Montreal *Gazette,* where he won a National Newspaper Award for critical writing, he has written three volumes of poetry, most recently *The Silver Palace Restaurant.* He has received both a Rhodes Scholarship and a Guggenheim Fellowship. Mark Abley lives in Pointe Claire, Québec.